GRAPHIC GREEK MYTHS AND LEGENDS

PERSEUS AND MEDUSA

By Nick Saunders
Consultant: Dr. Thorsten Opper, Curator of Greek
and Roman Antiquities, British Museum, London

WORLD ALMANAC® LIBRARY

Please visit our web site at: www.garethstevens.com
For a free color catalog describing World Almanac® Library's list of high-quality books and multimedia programs, call 1-800-848-2928 (USA) or 1-800-387-3178 (Canada). World Almanac® Library's fax: (414) 332-3567.

Library of Congress Cataloging-in-Publication Data available upon request from publisher. Fax (414) 336-0157 for the attention of the Publishing Records Department.

ISBN-13: 978-0-8368-7748-9 (lib. bdg.)
ISBN-13: 978-0-8368-8148-6 (softcover)

This North America edition first published in 2007 by
World Almanac® Library
A Member of the WRC Media Family of Companies
330 West Olive Street, Suite 100
Milwaukee, WI 53212 USA

This edition copyright © 2007 by World Almanac® Library. Original edition copyright © 2006 by ticktock Entertainment Ltd. First published in Great Britain in 2006 by ticktock Media Ltd.,Unit 2, Orchard Business Centre, North Farm Road, Tunbridge Wells, Kent, TN2 3XF

World Almanac® Library managing editor: Valerie J. Weber
World Almanac® Library art direction: Tammy West
Illustrators: Bookmatrix

Printed in Canada

1 2 3 4 5 6 7 8 9 10 10 09 08 07 06

CONTENTS

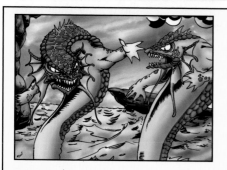

The world of the ancient Greeks was bound by the Mediterranean Sea and the rugged lands surrounding it. It was a place of dangerous winds and sudden storms. The ancient Greeks saw their lives as controlled by spirits of nature and the gods. They told myths about how the gods fought with each other and created the universe. These stories helped explain what caused natural events, such as lightning and earthquakes, and the fates of individuals.

The ancient Greeks believed that 12 gods and goddesses ruled over the world. The 10 gods and goddesses shown on the next page are the most important ones. Some of them appear in this myth.

The ancient Greek gods and goddesses looked and acted like human beings. They fell in love, were jealous and vain, and argued with each other. But unlike humans, they were immortal. They did not die but lived forever. They also had superhuman strength and specific magical powers. Each god or goddess controlled certain forces of nature or aspects of human life, such as marriage or hunting.

In the myths, the gods had their favorite humans. Sometimes, the gods even had children with these people. Their children were thus half gods. They were usually mortal, which meant that they could die. It also meant that they had some special powers, too. When their human children were in trouble, the gods would help them.

The gods liked to meddle in human life and took sides with different people. The gods also liked to play tricks on humans. They did so for many reasons—because it was fun; because they would gain something; or because they wanted to get even with someone.

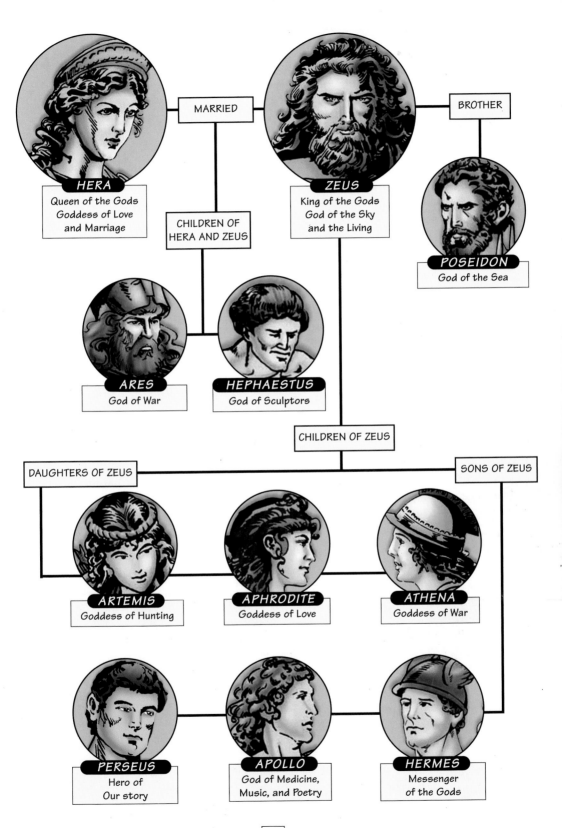

HERA
Queen of the Gods
Goddess of Love
and Marriage

MARRIED

ZEUS
King of the Gods
God of the Sky
and the Living

BROTHER

POSEIDON
God of the Sea

CHILDREN OF
HERA AND ZEUS

ARES
God of War

HEPHAESTUS
God of Sculptors

CHILDREN OF ZEUS

DAUGHTERS OF ZEUS

SONS OF ZEUS

ARTEMIS
Goddess of Hunting

APHRODITE
Goddess of Love

ATHENA
Goddess of War

PERSEUS
Hero of
Our story

APOLLO
God of Medicine,
Music, and Poetry

HERMES
Messenger
of the Gods

HOW THE MYTH BEGINS

The ancient Greeks loved good stories, especially ones that showed ordinary men winning great battles. The tale of Perseus killing the Gorgon Medusa showed the power of the immortal gods over human life. If someone honored the gods, the gods were good in return. If someone did not respect the gods, they would make that person's life very difficult.

When Medusa proudly claimed that she was more beautiful than Athena, the goddess of war swore to get revenge. So Athena helped the mortal Perseus kill Medusa. Perseus's life was glorious and tragic, but he was at last rewarded with everlasting fame.

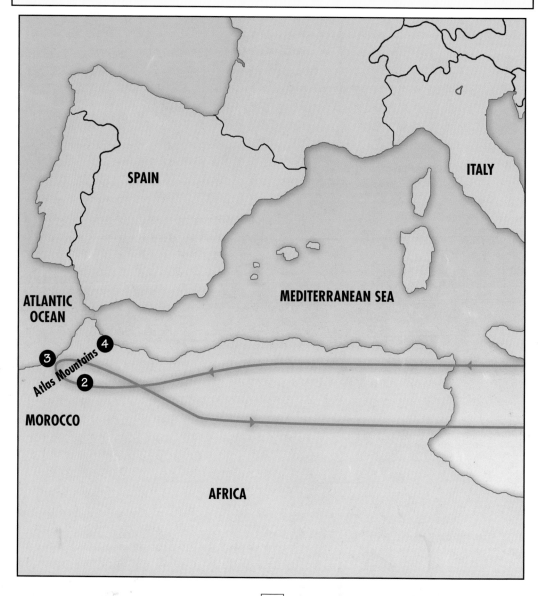

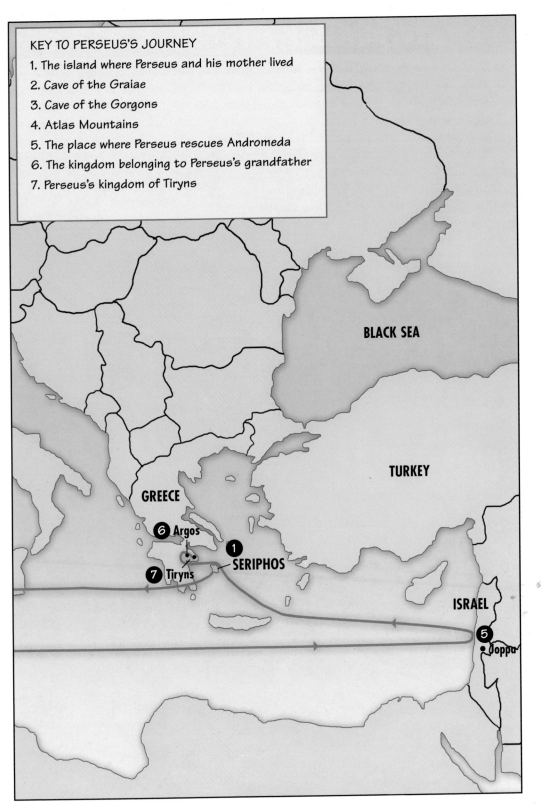

KEY TO PERSEUS'S JOURNEY

1. The island where Perseus and his mother lived
2. Cave of the Graiae
3. Cave of the Gorgons
4. Atlas Mountains
5. The place where Perseus rescues Andromeda
6. The kingdom belonging to Perseus's grandfather
7. Perseus's kingdom of Tiryns

BLACK SEA

TURKEY

GREECE

6 Argos

1 SERIPHOS

7 Tiryns

ISRAEL

5 Joppa

GORGONS AND GRAIAE

The hideous sea monsters Phorcys and Ceto had six evil daughters—the Gorgons and the Graiae. Each daughter looked frightening and had a special magical power. These horrible children lived on the very edge of the world, eating travelers who got lost.

The three Graiae lived in a cave on the western edge of the world. They were born looking like old, shriveled women with snakes for hair. They shared a single eye and just one tooth among themselves.

Enyo

Deino

Pemphredo

The Gorgon sisters also lived on the western edge of the world. Their cave was dark and filled with bones.

The Gorgons were the most sickening of Phorcys' and Ceto's children. They had razor-sharp claws and fierce, staring faces. Slithering snakes swarmed from their heads. Each also had a terrifying power. . . .

Our sisters, the Graiae, may think they are frightening. They are nothing compared to us!

Stheno **Medusa** **Euryale**

The first Gorgon was Stheno, meaning strength. She lived up to her name by lifting and throwing huge boulders.

No mortal man can match my strength. I can lift this rock as if it were a pebble.

Euryale also had a frightening power. She could leap across huge rivers and valleys. Euryale and her sister Stheno were immortal. They could not be killed.

Run! Run! You will not escape my mighty stride.

The third and most dangerous Gorgon was Medusa. She was a strange mix of beauty and evil. Unlike Stheno and Euryale, she was mortal and could be killed.

I may be mortal, but I am Queen of the Gorgons and the most deadly!

Sharp tusks pointed out from the corners of her mouth. A huge long tongue gave Medusa a gruesome look. Her blood was also a powerful poison.

No man can resist me. But they should watch out for the power of my eyes!

Medusa and Poseidon, the god of the sea, were lovers. They knew that the other gods wouldn't approve of their love because Medusa was so evil. So they met secretly in Athena's temple. Then Athena found out about the lovers!

14

To make matters worse, Medusa boasted that she was more beautiful than Athena. The goddess could not believe the pride of this hideous monster.

Oh "great" Athena! You are not as beautiful as I am! What god loves you as much as Poseidon loves me?

Medusa gave birth to Poseidon's child. Athena had had enough! The goddess was now determined that Medusa must pay for insulting her.

I swear by all the gods that you shall die for all these insults. I will find a hero to destroy you!

MAKING A HERO

The hero Athena found was the son of Zeus, king of the gods. A long time ago, Zeus had fallen in love with a beautiful woman, Danae. But Danae wasn't interested in Zeus. Each day Zeus watched Danae, longing to have a son with her. A son of whom he could be proud . . . a hero in the world of mortals.

So Zeus turned himself into a shower of golden rain. It fell from the clouds onto Danae's lap. Soon Danae found she was pregnant with Zeus's son.

I wonder where this glittering rain has come from? It sparkles like nothing I have seen before.

Athena was overjoyed when she found out that Danae would have Zeus's son. She knew that any son of Zeus would be strong and brave enough to kill a Gorgon.

Perseus! That would be a fine name for my son.

I will use Zeus's son to take my revenge on that foul creature Medusa!

Danae's father was King Acrisius, ruler of the city of Argos. Long ago, a seer had foreseen the king's future—and his death! The seer told the king that his own grandson would kill him.

Beware of Danae's son, he will kill you.

Can this be true? I must make sure this cannot happen.

When King Acrisius found out that Danae was pregnant, he locked her in a room, high in a tower with barred windows. Perseus was born in this prison, from which there was no escape.

What will I do? My son and I will be locked in this horrible place forever.

Within hours, King Acrisius's soldiers took Danae and Perseus to the shore. They forced the mother and child into a huge chest. The two were cast adrift on the sea . . . to die!

Push this chest out into the sea.

Perseus will drown and will not kill me!

Father . . . what are you doing?

Alone and scared, Danae was certain that she and her son would die.

Why has my father done such an awful thing to me?

King Acrisius didn't know that Zeus was protecting Danae and Perseus. The god of the sky kept them from drowning. He guided the winds so the chest drifted to the island of Seriphos.

I will always protect my son, Perseus. This island is a good place for him to grow up safely.

Zeus has saved us! But where are we?

As Danae carried her baby ashore, she was met by a kindly fisherman. He was the poor brother of King Polydectes, who ruled the island. When he heard Danae's story, he invited them to live with him in his small house.

Welcome to Seriphos, you poor creatures! My name is Dictys. Come inside and tell me your story.

Oh Dictys! May the gods bless you. We have been lost at sea.

King Polydectes heard of his brother's kindness. He insisted Danae and Perseus visit him. When they did, he fell in love with Danae's great beauty and kind nature.

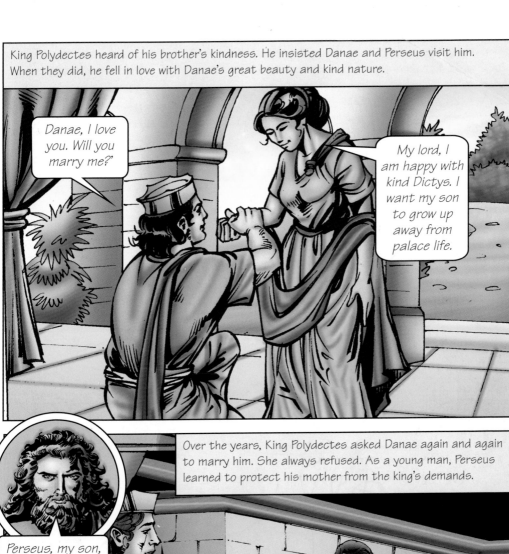

Danae, I love you. Will you marry me?'

My lord, I am happy with kind Dictys. I want my son to grow up away from palace life.

Over the years, King Polydectes asked Danae again and again to marry him. She always refused. As a young man, Perseus learned to protect his mother from the king's demands.

Perseus, my son, always protect your mother.

Danae! You know I love you. Why won't you become my queen?

My mother does not love you. Why don't you leave her alone?

King Polydectes was determined to marry Danae. But he knew that Perseus protected her. Her son would make sure the king left Danae alone. So he made up a new tax for all his people—to be paid in horses!

If you do not pay my tax, you and your mother must leave Seriphos!

You know it is impossible for me to pay your new tax. Neither my mother nor I have any horses. We are too poor.

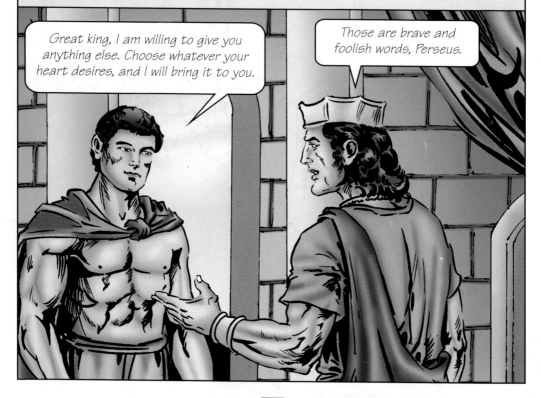

Unable to give King Polydectes any horses, Perseus made a desperate offer. To save himself and his mother, he promised to get anything that the king wanted.

Great king, I am willing to give you anything else. Choose whatever your heart desires, and I will bring it to you.

Those are brave and foolish words, Perseus.

Very well, stupid Perseus. I promise to leave your mother alone. In return, you must bring me the head of the Gorgon Medusa! Of course, you must kill her first.

How will I do that?

King Polydectes wants Medusa's head, does he? So do I!

Athena, help my son, Perseus, with his dangerous mission.

Perseus prepared as best he could for his mission. He had no idea how he would defeat the terrible Medusa. The night before he left, his sleep was restless and full of dreams about the goddess Athena. When he awoke, he found a shield beside him. Maybe this was a sign that the gods would look after him.

My brother, Hermes, and my friends, the Nymphs, will help you. But first you must find the Gorgons' sisters, the Graiae. Steal their eye and make them tell you where Medusa lives.

Hermes flew to Perseus's side. He guided him to the cave where the Graiae lived, high in the mountains at the western edge of the world.

There, Perseus! See that cave? That is where the three hags live.

Perseus crept silently into the dark cave, lit only by flickering torches. The three Graiae were asleep. He found their eye, grabbed it, and ran out of the cave.

After the Nymphs had left, Hermes returned. He also gave Perseus a gift. It was a huge, curved sword.

Perseus! Take this great blade. It is the sharpest sword that I have. With it, you can slice off Medusa's head.

There, lord Zeus, your son now has all he needs to defeat Medusa and save Danae.

Thank you, Hermes. I will put it to good use.

Athena, my daughter, you have done well!

This sword cuts through rock as though it's butter.

FINDING MEDUSA

Armed with his magical weapons and wearing his winged boots, Perseus flew to the western edge of the world. As he got closer, he saw the Gorgons' cave. He approached it carefully. He could see the statues of other men in the gloomy entrance. Would he survive the terrible Gorgons?

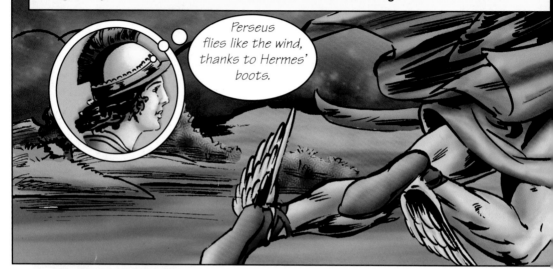

Perseus flies like the wind, thanks to Hermes' boots.

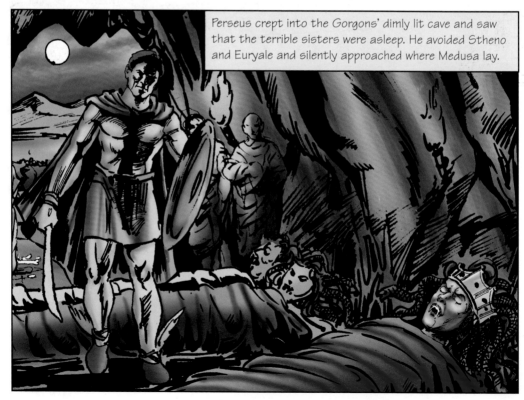

Perseus crept into the Gorgons' dimly lit cave and saw that the terrible sisters were asleep. He avoided Stheno and Euryale and silently approached where Medusa lay.

As he got closer to Medusa, Perseus carefully held up Athena's polished shield. He watched Medusa's reflection and resisted the urge to look at her directly.

Medusa suddenly awoke and leaped at Perseus. Guided by the reflection in his shield, Perseus raised the great curved sword and sliced off her head.

Careful not to look into Medusa's eyes, Perseus quickly stuffed her head into the bag that the Nymphs had given him.

Medusa's cries had woken her sisters, Stheno and Euryale. They flew at Perseus to tear him to pieces. But Perseus put on his magical cap. Instantly, he became invisible, then made his escape.

Euryale, run like the wind and catch our sister's killer!

Stheno! He has disappeared. I can't see him!

The Nymph's cap has saved me. These ugly sisters cannot see me!

Perseus lost the sisters and flew up into the sky. He was heading for home. Suddenly, a storm and strong winds filled the skies. They had been sent by the Titan Atlas. Atlas thought Perseus was looking for the precious golden apples that his daughters guarded.

What is happening? That mad Atlas, I'll punish him!

These apples belong to Hera, queen of the gods. I will kill anyone who tries to steal them, Perseus.

Atlas was a very powerful god whose family used to rule the heavens before Zeus. Not many people dared to fight Atlas.

Perseus became so angry at being blown around that he flew straight to Atlas. He pulled Medusa's head from the bag and held it up for Atlas to see.

Here, Atlas, look at this. You will never blow the winds again!

You can't scare me. It's only a head with some snakes . . .

When Atlas gazed at Medusa's eyes, he turned to stone.

Aaarrrggh! I can feel my limbs freezing. What is happening to me?

RETURNING HOME

Atlas's storm had blown Perseus far off course. He was a long way from home. As he flew toward land, he saw a beautiful woman chained to the edge of a cliff. Just then, Poseidon spoke to him. The god of the sea explained that the chained woman was Princess Andromeda, daughter of Cassiopea. Andromeda was being punished because her mother had insulted Poseidon's daughters.

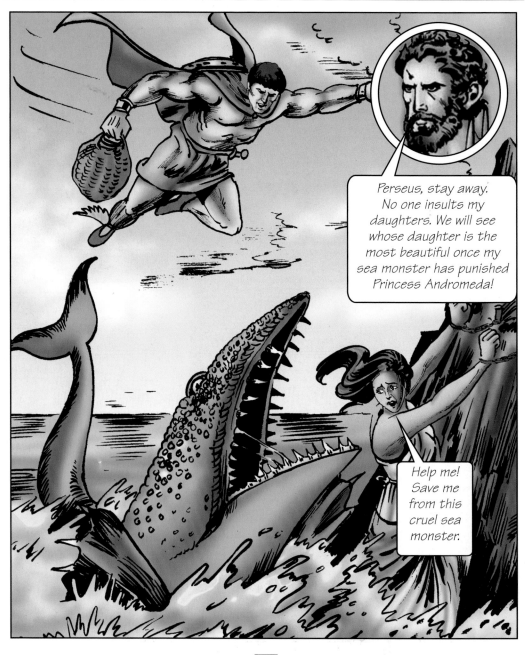

The hero Perseus could not stand by and watch as Andromeda died. He killed Poseidon's sea monster, broke Andromeda's chains, and flew away with her just in time.

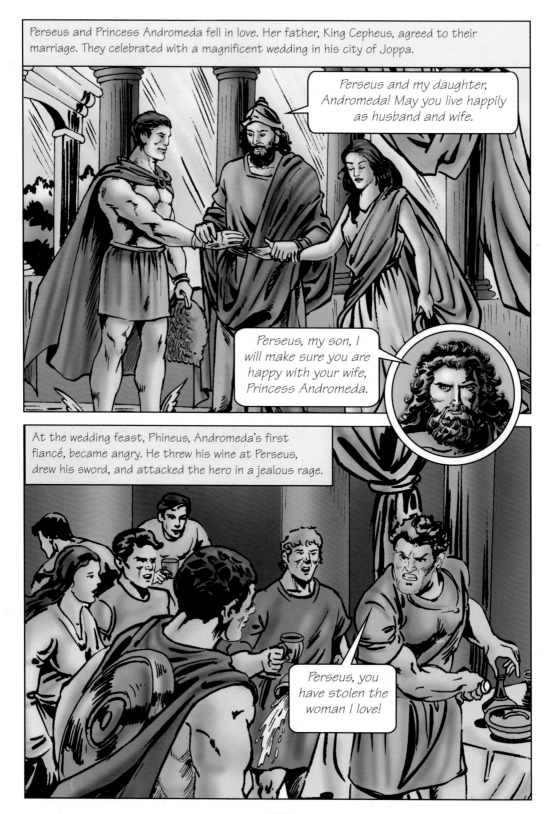

Perseus and Princess Andromeda fell in love. Her father, King Cepheus, agreed to their marriage. They celebrated with a magnificent wedding in his city of Joppa.

Perseus and my daughter, Andromeda! May you live happily as husband and wife.

Perseus, my son, I will make sure you are happy with your wife, Princess Andromeda.

At the wedding feast, Phineus, Andromeda's first fiancé, became angry. He threw his wine at Perseus, drew his sword, and attacked the hero in a jealous rage.

Perseus, you have stolen the woman I love!

The wedding guests screamed at Phineus to stop. He would not listen. Perseus quickly grabbed Medusa's head from his bag. He held it up to his attacker . . . turning Phineus to stone!

It was now time for Perseus and his new wife, Princess Andromeda, to continue their journey to the island of Seriphos. What would they find there?

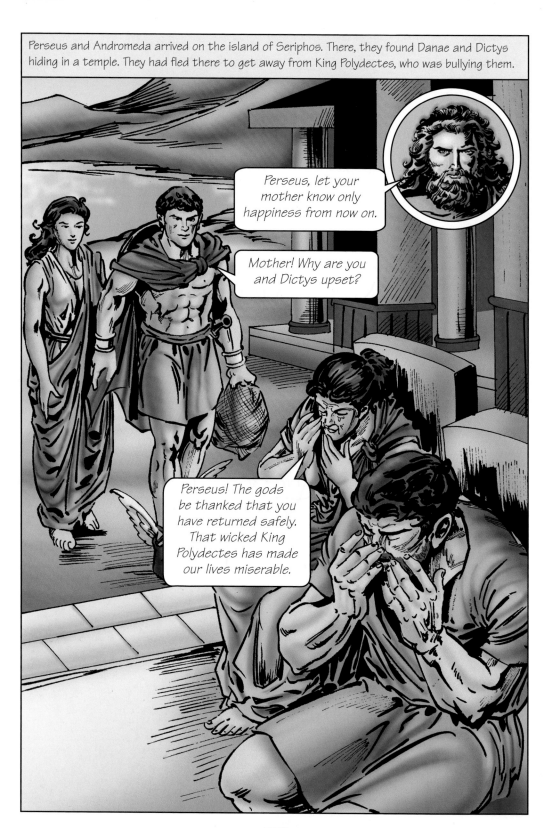

Perseus confronted King Polydectes. He told the king that he had finished his mission. He had killed the Gorgon, Medusa. King Polydectes laughed at Perseus.

Perseus was so angry that he opened the bag and pulled out Medusa's head. King Polydectes looked at it and was instantly turned to stone.

THE FINAL PROPHECY

Now that he had finished his mission and freed his mother, Perseus returned his magical weapons to Hermes and Athena. He also gave Medusa's head to Athena. She took the terrifying head and placed it on her armored breastplate to scare her enemies. What could be in store for Perseus now?

Perseus now took Andromeda to Argos to meet his grandfather, King Acrisius.

I can't wait to meet my grandfather.

Once in the city, the couple were told that the king was watching a sports competition. They went to find him there but found that it would be a while until the games were over. To pass the time, Perseus entered the discus contest. He threw with all his strength.

This man will surely win. Look at his strength and skill.

The discus has hit the king . . . he is dead!

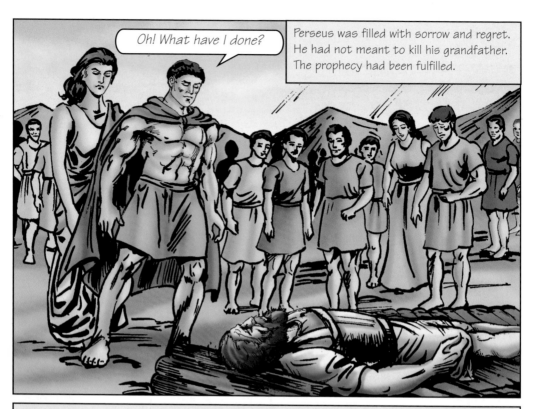

Soon, Perseus and Andromeda had a baby daughter. They named her Gorgophone, meaning "slayer of the Gorgon" in honor of Perseus.

Athena was grateful to Perseus for slaying Medusa. When he and his wife Andromeda died, the goddess turned them into stars to be seen in the night sky forever.

GLOSSARY

Argos *ancient city in southern Greece, ruled by king Acrisius. Perseus inherited it through his marriage to Acrisius's daughter Danae. When he accidentally killed Acrisius, Perseus arranged with Megapenthes to exchange the throne of Argos for Tiryns.*

Atlas *a Titan whose name means "he who carries;" in Greek myths, Atlas supported the sky*

Cassiopea *royal wife of King Cepheus of Joppa in Palestine (Israel). She angered Poseidon by boasting that her daughter Andromeda was more beautiful than his daughters, the Nereids.*

dreams *in ancient Greece, the gods spoke to mortals by appearing in dreams and visions, giving them advice*

discus *the bronze disc that was thrown during the Olympic Games in ancient Greece. The athlete who threw it farthest won the prize.*

fiancé *a man engaged to be married*

horses *a symbol of noble wealth in ancient Greece*

immortal *able to live forever, like the gods*

mission *an important job that is sometimes secret*

mortal *having a life that is ended by death*

Nymphs *the immortal daughters of Zeus, often shown as beautiful young women*

Phineus *royal brother of King Cepheus of Joppa in Palestine and the original fiancé of Andromeda*

prophecy *a statement about something that is going to happen in the future*

revenge *to get even for something done wrong to a person*

seer *a person who can see into the future*

Titan *a member of a race of gods who ruled the world before Zeus and his gods. They were giant creatures, the children of Uranus (Sky) and Gaia (Earth).*

BOOKS

Hepplewhite, Peter. *The Adventures of Perseus.* Ancient Myths (series). Minneapolis: Picture Window Books, 2004.

Lattimore, Deborah Nourse. *Medusa.* New York: HarperCollins Publishers, 2000.

McCaughrean, Geraldine. *Perseus.* Heroes (series). Peterborough, NH: Cricket Books, 2005.

Nardo, Don, and Bradley Steffens. *Medusa.* Monster (series). Farmington Hills, MI: KidHaven Press, 2004.

Spinner, Stephanie. *Snake Hair.* All Aboard Books Reading Level 2 (series). New York: Grosset & Dunlap, 1999.

WEB SITES

Make a Mask of Medusa
www.clemusart.com/kids/art/mask/index.html
Directions for making a mask of Medusa

Medusa the Gorgon: History for Kids
www.historyforkids.org/learn/greeks/religion/myths/medusa.htm
Short retelling—with a difference—of the story of Medusa and Perseus

Monstresses and Monstrosities
www.paleothea.com/LadyMonsters.html
Short descriptions of several female monsters from Greek myths, including Medusa

Publisher's note to educators and parents: Our editors have carefully reviewed these Web sites to ensure that they are suitable for children. Many Web sites change frequently, however, and we cannot guarantee that a site's future contents will continue to meet our high standards of quality and educational value. Be advised that children should be closely supervised whenever they access the Internet.

INDEX